Beckmann family.

THE STORY OF BRITAIN: BEFORE THE NORMAN CONQUEST

The author's lively approach to history and the artist's brilliant illustrations in both colour and black and white brings the past vividly to life in *The Story of Britain*, which was originally published as one volume.

The author, R. J. Unstead, is renowned as 'the young reader's historian'. He wrote his first book, *Looking at History*, when he was the headmaster of a school in Hertfordshire.

The artist, Victor Ambrus, has illustrated many books for children and has been awarded the Kate Greenaway Medal of the Library Association.

THE STORY OF BRITAIN:
BEFORE THE NORMAN CONQUEST

R. J. UNSTEAD

THE STORY OF BRITAIN: BEFORE THE NORMAN CONQUEST

Illustrated by Victor Ambrus

Carousel Editor: Anne Wood

TRANSWORLD PUBLISHERS LTD
A National General Company

THE STORY OF BRITAIN: BEFORE THE NORMAN CONQUEST

A CAROUSEL BOOK 0 552 54001 3

Originally published in Great Britain by
Adam and Charles Black Ltd.

PRINTING HISTORY
Adam and Charles Black edition (one volume entitled
The Story of Britain, which forms the Carousel edition
of *The Story of Britain: Before the Norman Conquest* and
the companion Carousel volumes *The Story of Britain:
In the Middle Ages, In Tudor and Stuart Times* and *From
William of Orange to World War II*) published 1969

Carousel edition published 1971
Carousel edition reprinted 1971
Carousel edition reprinted 1972

Text copyright © 1969 R. J. Unstead Publications Ltd.
Illustrations copyright © 1969 A. &. C. Black Ltd.

Carousel Books are published by Transworld
Publishers Ltd.,
Cavendish House, 57–59 Uxbridge Road,
Ealing, London, W.5

Made and printed in Great Britain by
Cox & Wyman Ltd., London, Reading and Fakenham

**NOTE: The Australian price appearing on the
back cover is the recommended retail price.**

CONTENTS

IN THE STONE AGE

ABOUT five thousand years before the birth of Christ a
neck of marshy land was flooded by sea, and Britain
became an island.

The islanders were few in number and their lives were
hard. By this time, the weather had grown wetter and
less cold than in the years of the great icefields, so the
land was covered by forests and the valleys were filled
with dense undergrowth and swamps. Only the chalk
hills and the windswept moors were open to the sky, for
there the soil was too thin for woodland trees.

Here and there, on the uplands and along the forest
edges, little groups of hunters tracked the wild boars, the
deer and the elk. They trapped some in pits and lamed

others with rocks. They followed the herds to cut off
strays and to run down the young ones, killing them
with flint hand-axes and sharp sticks.

When they killed, they ate, tearing the flesh with
teeth and fingers, cracking the bones for the marrow and
piercing the skulls to suck out the brains. Nothing was
wasted, for it might be days before they ate again. The
skins, the sinews and the needle-sharp bone-splinters had
their uses too.

These people lived where they could, in caves, in
cracks among the rocks and in pits piled round with
stones and roofed with boughs and turf. Their lives depended upon the animals that gave them food and cloth-

ing, and if the animals moved to fresh feeding-grounds
the hunter-families followed them.

But, in this bitter struggle to keep alive, man already
had his possessions. There were his weapons and scrap-
ers, his fire to keep him warm and to cook his meat and
his dogs to help him in the chase. So far, in Britain, he
had little else.

Away to the south and in the east, there were men
with many possessions. In Egypt, Mesopotamia, India
and China, where there was warmth and fertile soil
watered by great rivers, people were living in towns.
They had houses, temples and roads; they grew crops,
worshipped gods and were ruled by kings and priests.

Beyond the fertile valleys, the mountain folk and the herdsmen of the plains were on the move. From time to time they swept into the rich river-kingdoms and took them for their own. This surge of peoples in the east was like a sea whose waves flooded the empty lands. Its farthest ripples reached Britain before the island had a name.

Men from the Mediterranean lands moved up the coasts of Spain and France. There were always some who ventured a little farther than the rest, and presently a few bold fellows crossed the sea in their skin-covered boats and came to the southern and western shores of Britain. Others, from the northern plains, landed in the south-east and made their way inland along the grassy hills.

These newcomers understood the arts of weaving and pottery. They brought hoes and long-handled spades with which they could work the light soil of the hillsides, and they harvested their crops with flint sickles and ground the precious grain into flour. In addition they kept flocks and herds, and although they never lost their love of hunting, they no longer depended upon wild animals for all their food and their clothes.

Since animals had to be tended and guarded, the herdsmen-farmers made trenches and palisades to protect their flocks and also their homes. Settlements of round huts stood on the windy uplands of Salisbury Plain, the Chiltern Hills and Dartmoor, and near to the settlements great stones, called dolmens, were set up to please the spirits that caused the seed to sprout, and the lambs and the calves to be born.

Knowledge and skills were growing. Some men had special gifts and nimble fingers; they were the weavers, potters and artists; they chipped and polished the great flints dug out in underground galleries, they made tools and carved figures of the mother-goddess. A few were magic-men or priests. They knew how to make sacrifices to the spirits and the right way to bury the dead in hollow graves.

BEAKER FOLK AND CELTS

FROM about 2000 BC a new people began to arrive from eastern Europe. They were the Beaker Folk, whose name comes from the drinking vessels that they buried with their dead. They brought with them a knowledge of metals. Their bronze weapons and their bows and arrows gave them victory over the less well-armed people of the uplands. But there was room for both and the invaders mingled with the men they had conquered and married their daughters.

It was the Beaker Folk who raised the mysterious temples of Stonehenge and Avebury, those great circles of stones, some of which were dragged on rollers and floated down rivers for hundreds of miles. No one knows why these huge circles were made with so much effort.

Hundreds or even thousands of men must have laboured all their lives and have left the task to be finished by their grandsons. Stonehenge may have been a temple of the sun but we know next to nothing about the religion that drove men to such toil for their gods.

After the Beaker Folk, there were no more big invasions for several centuries; but from time to time small bands of settlers came to the western coasts, drawn perhaps by stories of Irish gold and Cornish tin whose fame had spread to Crete and Greece.

Then, from about 1000 BC, came the Celts, or Gaels, a fair-haired race who had crossed Europe and had given their name to Gaul. A few entered Britain. More joined them and then whole tribes came to settle in the south and the east, driving the inhabitants into the hills and forests of the west.

The Celts brought ploughs pulled by oxen and, from about 500 BC, their kinsmen arrived with weapons and tools of iron. Celtic smiths understood the secret of smelting ore in charcoal furnaces and their craftsmen

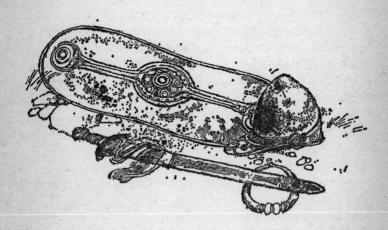

fashioned the metal into swords, into rims for shields and chariot-wheels, into fastenings for brooches and harness.

They were lively, quarrelsome, artistic people. Led by their warrior chiefs, the Celts defeated the islanders and fought among themselves in tribal wars, defending and attacking the huge earth fortresses that can still be traced on many hilltops. But they were also good farmers and business-men who used iron bars as money and set up a thriving trade in tin, lead, iron, corn and hides with the dark-faced merchants who came from the Mediterranean city-states.

One of these traders was Pytheas, a Greek from Massilia or Marseilles, who wrote a book about his voyage to the remote Tin Islands. In it, he described how Celts worked their tin-mines and brought the metal in wagons at low-tide to an island, probably St Michael's Mount, Cornwall, where the sea-traders came regularly to do business.

Above all, the Celts were artists in metal and precious stones. Their brooches, hand-mirrors, drinking-cups and even their helmets and shields were wonderfully shaped and decorated with circles and curving lines, with brilliant enamels and studded gems.

Vain, handsome, furiously proud, the Celts adored

finery and gaily coloured clothes. Men and women alike decked themselves with jewellery. They plaited and braided their long hair, smoothed it with combs and sometimes bleached it with chalk-wash to make themselves even fairer. The warriors took pride in their enormous moustaches and in the patterns that were painted on their bare chests before a battle.

These were the tribesmen whom the Romans fought. Their name, the Britons, came from one of the tribes called Brythons, but there were many others, the Iceni of East Anglia, the Brigantes and the Parisii in the north, the Cantii of Kent and the Belgae, a most powerful tribe who occupied nearly all the southern uplands from Sussex to Dorset. Though they were called Britons, they were not yet a nation, only a number of tribes in a wooded island where many of the earlier peoples still lived in the mountains.

JULIUS CAESAR IN BRITAIN

WHILE the Celts were raiding each other's hilltop forts and pushing into Ireland, Wales and the Scottish Highlands, a nation was growing from a handful of refugees who had built themselves a town on the banks of an Italian river. By nature and training, the Romans were conquerors. They defeated the Italian tribes, the Greeks, the mighty Carthaginians, the Spaniards and most of the peoples of the Middle East. When all the lands around the Mediterranean Sea were under their rule, the Romans pressed into Gaul, where the people were kinsfolk of the British tribes.

In the city of Rome, a pleasure-loving noble named Caius Julius Caesar bribed his way into the hearts of the common people. He gave them gifts and free circuses and they rewarded him with their cheers so that he became Consul for a year. After that, he was given command of the Roman Army in Gaul.

Although Caesar knew little about war until he was about forty, he swiftly proved himself one of the greatest generals in history. By 55 BC, he had conquered Gaul and had carried the Eagles across the Rhine to overcome the German tribes. After that, it was time, he thought, to pay a visit to the island whose shores could be seen from the coast of Gaul.

There were several reasons why the Roman general wanted to go to Britain. The tribesmen had been helping their friends in Gaul and many a defeated chief had escaped across the Channel. It seemed as if the islanders knew so little about the power of Rome that they were not at all frightened of Caesar and his legions. It was time they were taught a lesson and it would also be a fine thing to send messages to Rome with news of yet another triumph by the great general. Moreover, an expedition to Britain would fill the Roman citizens with pleasure and excitement.

The Tin Islands, wrapped in mist and peopled by giants and demons, had long fascinated the civilized world. It was said that there were fabulous riches in gold, tin and metals of every kind, besides unlimited crops of grain. If this were true, such riches must certainly be brought to Rome.

So, out of curiosity and military need, Caesar set sail from Gaul on an August evening in 55 BC. It was not a large force, but every man was a hardened soldier, well armed, well disciplined and absolutely confident of himself and his general. There was a force of cavalry, too, in boats broad enough to take the horses.

By morning, the Roman fleet was close to the shore of Britain. Ahead were towering cliffs where a landing was quite impossible. Caesar gave the order to sail along the coast until they came to a place where the cliffs gave way to a pebble beach. The captains were told to drive their vessels hard at the beach so that the soldiers could wade ashore.

This was done, but the men refused to jump. The shore was alive with British warriors who had followed along the cliffs and now were gathered in force upon the beach, yelling defiance and driving their war-chariots to the water's edge.

The Roman soldiers hated the sea and did not relish the thought of plunging in up to their armpits, to struggle through the waves towards a horde of painted savages. Besides, they had no knowledge of how to deal with chariots, a weapon of war that the Gauls had given up using.

At this moment, the Standard Bearer of the Tenth Brigade shouted, 'Jump, lads! I mean to do my duty. Follow me!' Holding aloft the pole that carried the silver Eagle, he plunged into the surf and the soldiers, fearing the disgrace of losing their precious Standard, leapt after him.

Men from the other ships followed their example and a fierce skirmish took place in the shallow water and along the shore. Gradually, the Romans got a footing on the beach, formed their ranks and pressed the Britons back until they scattered into the woods. There was no pursuit because the ships carrying the cavalry had not arrived. So the Romans made camp and waited for the morning.

Next day, messengers came from the British chiefs. They asked for peace and said that they would send handsome gifts if the Romans would go away. In reply, Caesar upbraided the Britons for ill-treating a messenger whom he had sent before the landing; the chiefs must send their men back to the fields while the terms of peace were being arranged.

Three days later, just as the ships carrying the cavalry were sighted, a storm blew up and once more forced them to return to Gaul. Worse than that, the fleet at anchor and the vessels that had been dragged a little way up the beach were badly damaged.

At once the Britons changed their attitude. They saw that Caesar was trapped. He could not sail back to Gaul and he had no stores to feed his men during the bad weather that lay ahead. There was no more talk of peace. The warriors looked to their arms and the chiefs sent word to their allies that they were gathering an army.

A sudden attack was made on Roman soldiers who had been sent out to collect corn. Hastily marching to their rescue, Caesar beat off the tribesmen and, as he retreated, he sent orders that every available man in camp was to set to work to repair the least-damaged ships with planks and nails from the wrecked vessels.

After one more skirmish, the Roman force embarked in the overcrowded ships and returned across the Channel to Gaul. It had been anything but a glorious expedition.

But Caesar was not the man to accept defeat. The bald, keen-eyed general kept his men at work all through the winter, and when summer came again he had a bigger fleet and a force specially trained to meet every danger and surprise.

This time there was no fight on the beach. The British chief, Cassivellaunus, had decided that he would draw the enemy inland and destroy him in the woods. So the Roman army landed without difficulty and, as usual, set to work to build a strong base camp.

Leaving a force to guard the ships and the stores, Caesar advanced warily. His cavalry probed ahead to view the unknown countryside and to search out the tribesmen. The Britons held off. Sometimes they swooped along the enemy's flanks or darted out of ambushes, but they refused to fight a pitched battle.

The Roman legions marched on grimly until they came to the River Thames. Here the Britons held a ford in strength but, after a bitter engagement, the Romans forced their way across. Cassivellaunus rallied his warriors but the remorseless enemy pressed them back into Hertfordshire where the British stronghold was taken by storm.

The Britons lost heart. So many of the tribesmen offered to surrender that Cassivellaunus had to ask for

peace. Caesar readily agreed. Already he was anxious to
return to Gaul, for news had come that the whole
country was about to burst into rebellion as the Gallic
chiefs made a last effort to win back their freedom.

Caesar had given the Britons a taste of Rome's power.
That was enough for the present. With promises of tri-
bute and a few hostages of noble birth, he hurried away
to crush the Gauls and, later, to make himself master of
the Roman world. In the years of struggle and triumph
that followed, he had no time to spare a thought for the
remote island where he had so narrowly escaped disaster.

THE ROMAN CONQUEST

NINETY years passed before the legions came back to Britain. By that time, however, Roman ideas and Roman goods were well known in the southern part of the island.

Gaul had developed into a splendid province, with wide cornfields and busy towns. Merchants crossed to Britain to sell their wares for tin and iron and slaves. Kinsmen travelled to and fro and more Belgic tribes came across to settle, bringing new ideas and heavy ploughs that could bite into the lowland clay.

Some of the British chiefs began to live in the style that the newcomers talked about. They wore dignified robes and had gold coins made with Latin words on them; they called themselves kings and believed that their courts were every bit as sumptuous as the Emperor's. Visitors hid their smiles and agreed that the thatched huts at Camulodunum (Colchester), capital of Cassivellaunus' grandson, Cunobelin, were as splendid as the buildings in Rome itself.

The Romans had not forgotten the name of Britain. To them, with their tidy minds and sense of order, it was not right for these half-barbaric islanders to imitate Roman ways and to boast of their freedom. When someone had time and an army to spare, Britain must be brought into the Empire. Caligula planned an invasion but he was a madman who changed his mind, so the task fell to the Emperor Claudius, a sickly, bookish man who wanted a conquest that was not too difficult.

In AD 43 an army of some 40,000 men under Aulus Plautius landed in Kent. Following Caesar's line of advance, it forced its way across the Medway and the Thames into the strongest part of the island. The Emperor himself arrived to encourage his troops by his presence and to dismay the Britons by the sight of his military elephants.

Camulodunum was captured and eleven chiefs were brought to make their surrender to the Emperor. They were told that their capital would be rebuilt in the Roman style with a temple in honour of Claudius as its centre-piece. They and their people were now subjects of Rome but, if they behaved themselves and paid their taxes, they would enjoy the blessings of trade and law.

After Claudius had gone back to his books in Rome, the legions set about conquering the whole island. It was not as easy as they had thought. The half-civilized south-east had surrendered readily, for the chiefs knew and admired the power of Rome, but inland, in the west and the north, there were tribes that cared nothing for tiled pavements and elegant robes. Moreover, Caradoc or Caractacus, son of Cunobelin, was made of braver stuff than many of the chiefs.

He refused to surrender and moved into the west where he rallied the hill-tribes who lived by rough farming and robbery. Here, in Wales, Caractacus fought the legions for eight years, always losing ground but never giving up the struggle. At last the Romans brought him to bay in a hill-fort called Caer Caradoc – the fort of Caractacus. His army was destroyed but he escaped to the Brigantes, only to be betrayed into the hands of the conquerors.

Taken to Rome and paraded in chains through the streets for the amusement of a gaping crowd, Caractacus so impressed the spectators by his upright dignity that they forgot to jeer. Looking about at the lofty buildings, Caractacus cried out to his fellow-captives, 'Why did the Romans rob us of our huts when they have houses like these?'

The Emperor was astonished by the prisoner's bold gaze. 'Do you not know, Briton, that you are about to die?' he asked.

Caractacus looked up at him. 'I did not fear death in battle against your soldiers. Why should I fear it here? Put me to death, Emperor. I shall soon be forgotten. Spare my life and it is you who will be remembered!'

'Strike off his chains,' cried the Emperor. 'Rome knows how to pardon a brave enemy.'

Caractacus was said to have settled in Rome with his

family. Another story said that he returned to Britain to his estates. If he did, he would have found that his countrymen were far from happy.

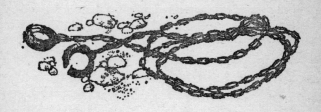

BOADICEA'S REBELLION

THE tribes had surrendered but where, they asked, was the good life promised by the Romans? Bullying officials demanded gifts and heavy taxes to pay for the troops, the fortified towns and the long straight roads. The Britons grew sullen and their anger was fanned by their priests, the Druids, many of whom had retreated to the dense thickets of the holy island of Mona or Anglesey.

The main Roman army was on its way to Anglesey to destroy the sacred groves when, in the year AD 61, a great rebellion broke out in the east.

Enraged by tax-officials who had brutally insulted Queen Boadicea and her daughters, the Iceni tribe of East Anglia took up arms. They killed the officials and were speedily joined by a host of warriors from neighbouring tribes.

Led by their tall, handsome Queen, the Britons swept

down upon the new towns, shrieking their battle-cry, 'Death to the Romans!'

The hated temple of Claudius at Camulodunum was torn down, Verulamium (St Albans) was savagely destroyed and its inhabitants massacred, the Ninth Legion was overwhelmed and the port of Londinium went up in flames.

News of these frightful happenings reached Paulinus, the Roman Governor, as he was nearing the stronghold of the Druids. Immediately he ordered his army to turn about and march south to seek out the rebels.

A vast host of Britons had gathered to destroy their enemy. So certain were they of victory that they had brought their wives and children to watch the battle from the lines of wagons piled high with plunder from the looted towns.

Paulinus took up a strong position and looked calmly across at Boadicea's great force of wildly excited tribesmen.

'Men,' he cried, 'today we fight for Rome and for life itself. There can be no retreat. Stand firm. Keep your ranks. Bear yourselves like soldiers of your legion. These are savages led by a woman!'

From her chariot, Boadicea also addressed her army. She reminded them that once they had been free. Now they were slaves. But they had shown that they could beat the Romans. One more victory and all was won.

'Death to the Romans! Drive them into the sea!'

The Britons answered with a great shout and charged. They hurled themselves against the Roman shields, battering with maddened courage a foe that was better armed, better led and grimly cool. The Romans held their ranks and then, as the charges grew less furious, they advanced in line, step by step, pressing the Britons back to the wagon-lines where they slaughtered them beside the plundered wealth.

In a woodland clearing, Boadicea and her daughters drank poison to escape a more horrible death. The revolt was over.

AGRICOLA

ON that day a young officer named Agricola fought in the army of Paulinus. Afterwards he saw service in other parts of the Empire and, seventeen years later, he came back as Governor of Britain.

Agricola had not forgotten the islanders' bravery nor the reasons why they had rebelled. He knew that they still hated the Romans but he vowed to give them peace and justice.

First he had to deal with the Druids who were still causing trouble. Then, after he had destroyed them and all their holy places, he conquered Wales and turned his attention to the Picts who lived in Caledonia or Scotland.

Although Agricola defeated the Picts, he found it impossible to carry on winter warfare in the northern forests and highlands. So he built a line of forts to keep the

savage tribes in check while he took up the task of
changing the rest of Britain into a civilized province.

For the Romans, civilization meant living in a town. A
town was easy to rule; townsmen could be counted and
taxed, their comings and goings were known, their work
was buying and selling, hammering, writing and carrying, instead of hunting and fighting.

More than fifty towns were built in Britain, neat
towns with straight streets crossing at right-angles, with
temples, law-courts, shops, market-places and public
baths. Often they were built near the site of an old settle-
ment or at a ford or at a place where roads crossed and
where it was natural for people to gather for trade or
safety. In timber and brick, with thatched and tiled
roofs, with pavements and stone pillars, towns went up
all over Britain from York and Lincoln in the north, to

T–B

Chester and Caerleon on the Welsh frontier, to Bath, Exeter, Dorchester, Winchester and London.

In the south, retired officials and former chiefs owned large corn-growing estates known as villas, where the nobility lived in centrally-heated comfort, waited upon by trained slaves.

As time went by, many Britons were proud to be citizens of Rome. They dressed in the toga, sent their sons to school and sat with their elegant wives at the theatre or the games. Humbler townsfolk followed their daily occupations and spent their wages in the market and the wine-shop just like the townspeople in Gaul or Spain or any other part of the Empire.

THE EMPEROR HADRIAN

IN Roman Britain there was always the feeling of living on the very edge of the civilized world. In Wales and Cornwall and on the northern moors, the hill people still jeered at Roman law and clung to their old tribal ways. Sea-pirates from Ireland sometimes came ashore to rob and to snatch a few captives to sell to the slave-merchants.

The Picts of Caledonia were never subdued for long, and every now and then they broke through the line of forts to burn and slay and to take as much plunder as they could carry.

It was one of these raids that brought the Emperor Hadrian to Britain in AD 121. The Ninth Legion had been ordered out from York to pursue and punish the robbers. Somewhere in the wild north, the legion met disaster. Trapped perhaps in a glen, led into an ambush by a false guide or simply overwhelmed by a blizzard, the Ninth vanished with its Eagle Standard.

Hadrian landed at the port of Richborough in Kent. Escorted by the Sixth Legion from Germany, he marched up through the peaceful countryside, noting with approval its rich cornlands and prosperous towns. At York the garrison was paraded and drilled before the Emperor's unsmiling gaze and, when he was satisfied with its performance, he chose a strong company to march with him into Scotland. He would see for himself the country whose tribesmen refused to be conquered.

This Hadrian was a strange man. Brought up in Spain, educated in Rome and Athens, he had fought in wars against Rome's eastern enemies and had travelled with his uncle, the Emperor Trajan, more widely than any other Roman alive. When Trajan died, Hadrian became Emperor but, after he had made his position safe in Rome by favouring the common people and killing off his enemies, he set out again on his travels.

Sometimes on horseback but usually on foot, Hadrian visited Parthia, Syria, Egypt, Spain, Gaul and Germany. By the time he reached Britain, he was quite certain that the Empire was big enough. Rome needed no more conquests but strong frontiers to keep the barbarians out. So everywhere he ordered walls, fortresses and defence lines to be built. Behind them there was to be peace, for the Emperor Hadrian was more than an able general. He loved music and painting. He wrote poetry and built libraries, theatres and temples. And he cared deeply about the people whom he ruled with justice and generosity, though they never understood him, for he seldom spoke and he would sometimes behave with horrible cruelty.

At a speed that exhausted his toughest soldiers, Hadrian surveyed the land of the Picts, walking and climbing in rough country, studying maps and measurements, as he snapped instructions to his weary officers. Then he called his Staff together and pointed to a map.

'You will build a wall,' he said, 'from here to here.

That is the shortest distance between the seas. It measures seventy-six miles. The wall is to be ten feet thick and twenty feet high. There will be a ditch in front thirty feet wide and you will place forts, signal-posts and gates for peaceful traffic. Let it be done with speed. Your task is to put an end to these raids. In my Empire there must be peace.'

The work took five years. Ten thousand soldiers dug the earth and raised the stones until Hadrian's Wall stretched from coast to coast. It was the mightiest fortification ever built in Britain. On its top it was wide enough for two soldiers to march abreast, and, at one-mile intervals, there were 'mile castles', besides seventeen large forts to house the garrison troops.

THE END OF ROMAN RULE

THE Wall so disheartened the Picts that, twenty years later, a second wall, this time made of turf, was built farther north between the Forth and the Clyde. But the new frontier could not be held. In AD 190 some of the Roman troops were withdrawn from Britain and at once the Picts broke out, crossed the Scottish Lowlands, forced their way over Hadrian's Wall and went plundering far into Roman Britain.

The Emperor Severus came to drive the Picts back. He retook Hadrian's Wall and made it stronger, besides rebuilding the city of Eboracum, or York, which had been burnt to the ground. But there was no second at-

tempt to push any farther into Scotland. The Wall was the frontier and the soldiers who were stationed there and who retired from their service to live nearby, were guarding the most northerly outpost of the Empire.

For another century Britain enjoyed peace, but by the year 300 small fleets of raiders from Germany were regularly attacking the coasts. They came ashore to rob and slipped away as soon as armed forces appeared. These Saxons became such a nuisance that the Romans had to build forts all along the coast from Norfolk to the Isle of Wight. In command of these defences was an officer known as the Count of the Saxon Shore.

Rome's difficulties increased. Every frontier was threatened by barbarians pressing in to enjoy the riches of a vast Empire. In Rome itself there was no longer the heart and will to put right the things that were wrong.

Emperors came and went. Sometimes there were rival Emperors who fought each other for power, sometimes a strong Emperor checked the barbarians for a time and tried to reform the taxes, but after he went decay set in again.

In 367 the Picts broke into Britain again and destroyed the legion at York; the Saxon raids increased, Irish sea-pirates landed in the west and thousands of slaves snatched their freedom and joined in plundering the undefended towns.

Then there was a recovery. Law and order were restored and the legions stood on guard once more. But in 410 the Emperor sent a message to the Britons, telling them that they must defend themselves. He needed the legions to save the city of Rome.

So the Roman army sailed from Britain in the year when Alaric and his Visi-Goths sacked the capital of the world. Steadily, Roman Britain crumbled into ruins.

THE STORY OF ST ALBAN

IN the 350 years during which the Romans ruled Britain, they brought many blessings and new ideas. To a semi-barbaric land, they gave roads, towns, education, law and improved ways of farming. Nearly all of these vanished after the Romans left, although the roads lasted longest and were later rebuilt, with many of the towns.

But one gift did not disappear. It was the Christian religion. When the Romans first came, they brought their beliefs in the old gods such as Jupiter, Mars and Diana. Then Emperors were raised to the level of gods and religions from the conquered lands gained favour – there was the goddess Isis from Egypt and Mithras, an eastern god who was popular with soldiers.

Steadily, secretly, because it was often forbidden, a new religion called Christianity made its way into Britain. Its message of hope appealed strongly to poor people and to slaves, but there were powerful persons who disliked a religion that acknowledged only one god.

Most people in the Ancient World accepted the various gods who belonged to different towns, rivers and holy places. It was their refusal to accept any other god, even the Emperor, that led the Christians into trouble. At times they were left in peace, but at others they were hunted down, tortured and put to death. Yet, no matter how they were treated, their religion spread and it took root in Britain.

In about the year 300, a young man named Alban lived in the Roman town of Verulamium. He had been born in Britain but his father was rich enough to send him to school in Rome, and later he had served his time in the army, as befitted a gentleman of means and birth. Now he was living in a fine house in his home town where he was well liked for his kind deeds and for his generosity to the poor.

One day Alban arrived home to find an old man resting in his porch. He was obviously exhausted and near to collapse. Alban carried the stranger into his house,

gave him food and drink and told him to rest until he felt stronger.

Presently the old man explained that his name was Amphibalus and that he was a Christian priest wanted by the Roman officials for preaching the forbidden religion. Hunted by soldiers, he had lost touch with his friends, some of whom had already been put to death. After wandering from place to place he had come to seek shelter in Alban's house.

'But why did you come to me?' cried Alban. 'I am a Roman citizen, obedient to the law.'

'I know that,' replied the old man. 'I also know that you are a good man, a helper of the needy and the poor. I beg you to help me until I am strong enough to go out and preach the Word.'

By this time the old priest was too weak to be asked any more questions, so Alban put him to bed in an inner room where, unknown to the servants, he looked after him for many days.

As Amphibalus grew stronger, he and Alban often talked together. The young man asked questions about a religion that men would die for and, as the priest explained the teachings of Jesus, Alban became certain that this was indeed the true religion. He asked Amphibalus to teach him how to enter the Christian faith.

One morning, when they were praying together, a servant came running to tell Alban that he had heard that soldiers were on their way to search the house. A Christian was said to be hiding there.

Alban acted quickly. He told the old man to exchange his shabby robe for some of his own clothes, to wrap himself in a warm cloak and, with a purse of money, to make his way to a place of safety. When he had received the priest's blessing, he hurried him to a side-gate and, telling him that he would delay the soldiers somehow, bid his friend farewell.

Minutes later soldiers stormed into the house and discovered a man kneeling in prayer in an inner room. Seeing that he was dressed in the robe and hood of a Christian priest, they dragged him out and took him to the Governor.

When the prisoner's hood was thrown back, everyone in the court-house saw to their astonishment that it was Alban, one of their best-known citizens. The Governor was very angry at the trick that had enabled the priest to escape but he knew that Alban was a man of good birth and reputation. For the sake of his father, an old friend, he would pardon this piece of folly. Of course, Alban must make the proper offerings to the Roman gods.

'I cannot do that,' said Alban, 'I am a Christian and I know that there is only one God.'

His friends and even the Governor pleaded with him but he refused to deny his religion. In accordance with the law, he was sentenced to death.

The soldiers marched Alban out of the town to the place of execution on a hill. So great was the crowd that it was impossible to pass over the bridge across the river, but when the soldiers thrust their prisoner down the bank to make him wade across, it was said that the waters miraculously dried up. It was said, too, that when, before his death, Alban asked for a drink, a clear spring gushed out of the ground and was known as Holywell ever afterwards.

Having heard Alban pray for those who were about to execute him, the soldier who was detailed to kill him flung down his sword, saying that he would not strike a holy man. At this, the officer in charge snatched up the weapon and killed both Alban and the soldier.

In later years, when the Christian faith was no longer persecuted, a church was built on the hill where the first British martyr died and, as the Roman town fell into ruins, the new town by the church was called St Albans.

HOW ST PATRICK CONVERTED
IRELAND

NOT long after St Alban's death, the Emperor Constantine became a Christian and his religion spread rapidly through many parts of the Empire. In Britain we know that the faith reached far into the west country and the north.

It was somewhere in western Britain, perhaps in Glamorganshire or as far north as the banks of the Clyde, that a boy named Patrick was brought up on a farm near the coast. These were troubled times, for the end of Roman rule was not far off, but the boy's parents were good Christians and his father, besides being a farmer, was a deacon of the Church.

One day, when Patrick and his friends were playing on the shore, they were surprised by a band of Irish pirates who had come ashore unnoticed. Before the lads could get away they were overpowered and thrust aboard the pirates' boat, which carried them to Northern Ireland.

Patrick was sold to an Ulster chieftain who put him to work on the land. The boy was lonely and homesick but he pluckily made the best of his hard life. He learned to speak the Irish language and found that, although the people were heathens, they were good-hearted in a rough, half-savage way. Every day, when he was alone with his master's flock, Patrick prayed to God for courage and patience, for he was certain that help would come to him.

After six years as a slave, Patrick ran away and made his way to the coast. Here he came across a ship about to sail to Britain with a number of Irish wolfhounds which always fetched a good price. The captain promised to give him a passage if he would help to mind the fierce animals. Patrick joyfully agreed for he knew, from his years on the farm, that he had a strange power to make creatures obey him. The sailors watched in astonishment when the great hounds followed him quietly on board.

The ship had not been long at sea before a storm blew up and the steersman could only run before the wind while the crew bailed hard all night long. After several days, when the wind dropped, the sailors found that they were off the coast of Gaul. Patrick was by now a favourite with the crew and they agreed to set him ashore to try to find his way home.

Months later, Patrick reached the farmstead where he was born. His parents and his brothers were overjoyed to see him for they had long believed him to be dead. He settled happily at the farm for a time but in his heart he knew that he could not stay there.

Now that he had seen something of the world, Patrick was sure that a great task was waiting for him but, as yet, he did not know where it lay. One night he dreamed that a man came to him with a message: at first he could not understand it until he heard voices saying, 'Come back and walk among us as before.' Then he could see the fields and woods where he had served as a slave. When he awoke he knew what he must do.

He said good-bye to his family and made his way to Gaul. At length he came to the monastery at Tours where he had been given shelter on his way home. When he explained that he wished to be trained to be a priest in order to carry the Word of God to the Irish, the Prior

welcomed him in. He would have to prove himself
worthy to join the brotherhood of monks, and after that
there would be a long training, but God would decide all
things.

For seventeen years Patrick worked at this monastery
and at another in Gaul, carrying out the duties and services of a monk, studying the Bible and preparing himself for the task that he hoped to undertake. At last he
was made a bishop and given permission to go to Ireland.

With a small band of monks, Patrick landed on the
coast that he had first seen from a pirate galley. He went
to the place where he had worked as a slave, only to find
that his old master was dead and his friends scattered.
The people were far from friendly, but Patrick strode to
the Hall of their Chief, who was at dinner with his
household.

'Hear me, O Chief,' cried Patrick, 'I bring news that
is worth telling.'

Surprised to hear himself addressed in the Irish
language, the Chief told the stranger to speak on.
Patrick then described his adventures and dreams. He
said that God had directed him to Ireland to lead its
people out of their ignorance to knowledge of the true
God.

When he had ended, the Chief bade Patrick to be
seated with his followers. They must eat and drink, for
they were his guests, and later he would hear more of
this new religion.

From that day Patrick made headway. Despite the
anger of the Druids, the Chief became his loyal friend
and was the first to be baptized. He gave the monks a
piece of land on which to build their huts and a small
wooden church.

Patrick travelled to all parts of Ireland, preaching,

baptizing and training men to continue his work. Where-ever he went, he left monks to build a church so that, when, after many years of ceaseless activity, Patrick died in the green land that he loved, Ireland was a Christian country. By this time, however, Christianity had almost disappeared in the rest of Britain.

THE ANGLES AND SAXONS

AFTER the Romans went away, there was a long period lasting for more than 150 years which is known as the Dark Ages. This is a period of history about which we know very little. It was a time of fighting and destruction, when homes, belongings and writings were burnt and people left no record of their lives.

It seems certain that, as soon as the legions sailed away, the Picts and the Welsh came swarming in to rob and kill with little fear of being driven back to their hills. Naturally the Britons defended themselves. They had weapons and many were rich, with servants and guards.

Life went on fairly well in some of the towns far from the hills, but gradually the whole system that the Romans had built fell to pieces. There was no one to take command, to fix the taxes, to organize the everyday business of town and country. Trade, law and order came to a standstill. Townspeople found that their work had gone; some doubtless went back to the land, some tried to carry on as best they could in the dying towns and some joined the robber-bands that roved the country.

To defend their homes, men joined themselves to local leaders and soon there were petty wars, as the nobles fought for power and land.

Out of these struggles, a nobleman, Vortigern, rose to be the strongest leader of the Britons. But even he could not find enough fighting-men to keep the Picts in check. They came robbing and burning as far south as Kent and, since it was hopeless to ask the Romans for help, Vortigern thought of a plan to drive the tribesmen back. He would invite the Saxons to come across the sea to fight in his army for pay; they were splendid warriors and would be more than a match for the Picts.

The Saxons eagerly accepted the invitation and came to serve in Vortigern's army under their chiefs, Hengist and Horsa, two valiant brothers who quickly realized that this fertile land was far better than their own bleak homeland.

By the time Vortigern realized the danger, the Saxons were strong enough to defy him. It is said that Horsa was slain in a battle but Hengist took the land of Kent and made it his own kingdom.

This success brought more Saxon war-bands to the island. There was no great invasion, only a steady stream of landings, as the curved boats came up the rivers and the invaders went ashore to pillage the farms and the almost deserted towns. Wives and sturdy blue-eyed children followed the warriors, who seized farm-lands and settled down under their chiefs, as ready to plough as to fight.

Although they were called Angles, Saxons and Jutes, the invaders were one race, speaking a common language and ready to band together whenever the Britons made a stand.

The islanders did not give in easily. For a hundred years they fought hard, and from time to time a leader would arise to give them hope. Arthur was one of the British chiefs whose victories over the heathens were sung and re-sung until they became a legend of a hero-king who sat with his knights at a round table in a vanished kingdom.

But if the invaders were sometimes defeated in a battle, they were never mastered or driven out. Always they regathered their forces to drive the Britons a little farther back into Devon, Cornwall, Wales and south-west Scotland.

By the year 600 the pagan Anglo-Saxons were masters of all but the hilly rain-swept fringes of Britain and the country was called England, the land of the Angles.

ST COLUMBA AND ST AUGUSTINE

THE invaders were tribal warriors. They fought under their chiefs and settled the land, piece by piece, under their rule. So a number of separate kingdoms emerged, some of them no bigger than a modern county, as Essex, the kingdom of the East Saxons, and Sussex, kingdom of the South Saxons. Some of the other heathen realms were Kent, Northumbria, Mercia, Wessex and East Anglia.

Thor, Woden and Freya were the stark gods that the conquerors worshipped and, after death – more honourable in battle than in bed – the warriors hoped for an after-life of feasting in the halls of Valhalla.

But beyond these kingdoms, Christianity lived on among the Celtic people of Wales and the west. Thanks to St Patrick, it flourished in Ireland, where monks chanted their services and copied their manuscripts with loving care. So far, however, no one tried to win the Angles away from their terrible idols.

It was a quarrel over a book borrowed by one Irish monastery from another that caused Columba to make his missionary journey in AD 563. Men were killed in the quarrel and Columba, Abbot of Derry, vowed to go across the sea to win more souls for God than had been lost in the squabble.

In a tiny boat he sailed to Iona, an island off the south-west coast of Scotland, where he and twelve brother-monks built a church and a group of huts.

When he had founded the monastery, Columba made a perilous journey to the mainland and across country to the court of King Buda, ruler of the Northern Picts. Here he was able to convert the fierce tribesmen to Christianity.

As a result, Iona became the religious centre of the north at a time when the Christians in Britain were cut off from the rest of the world and knew nothing of what was happening in Gaul and Rome.

It had been an unknown Roman soldier who had first brought the Christian religion to Britain and now it was a Roman priest who vowed to restore the faith to the southern part of the island.

When St Columba was baptizing the Picts, a young priest named Gregory was walking through the slave market of Rome, where captives from all over Europe

were brought to be sold. He paused to look at these be-
wildered men and women of all races, when his attention
was caught by a group of fair-haired, blue-eyed children.

'Who are these beautiful children?' he asked the slave-
merchant.

'They are Angles,' replied the man.

'Angles?' said Gregory. 'They look more like angels
from Heaven itself.'

Gregory asked the Pope for permission to take the
Gospel to a land that produced such splendid people, but
the Pope had other tasks for him to do.

Years passed and Gregory became Pope. He had
never forgotten that group of forlorn children in the
market and he chose a prior named Augustine for the
mission that he had longed to carry out.

With forty monks Augustine travelled across Gaul,
but, as they came nearer to Britain, they heard at every
monastery where they lodged such terrifying stories of
the heathen Angles that their courage failed. The
monks begged Augustine to go back to the Pope to tell
him that the task was impossible.

Gregory put new heart into Augustine who, in his
turn, was able to persuade the monks to go forward,
placing their trust in God. Besides, he had one piece of
comforting news. Queen Bertha, wife of the King of
Kent, was the daughter of the Count of Paris and she
had been brought up as a Christian. Although she had
had no success in converting her husband, she had managed to send word that a party of missionaries might
succeed where she had failed. At least, she would do her
best to see that they were not ill-treated.

In 597 the missionaries' boat grounded its keel in a
sandy bay of Thanet. With the Cross at their head and
with one of their number carrying a large picture of

Jesus, the monks moved inland to the place where King Ethelbert had consented to meet them, with his Queen and nobles.

They met in the open air, the King seated under an oak-tree, for it was feared that the strangers might work magic indoors. Augustine stepped forward and spoke earnestly about the life and teachings of Jesus.

The King listened intently, but he was very cautious. 'Your meaning is not clear to me,' he said. 'But you seem to be good men and you have travelled far to speak in this fashion. You may stay here without hurt, and speak to any who will hear you.'

Queen Bertha was delighted. The King had earlier given her the half-ruined Roman church of St Martin, on the outskirts of Canterbury. Now she could invite the monks to make their homes there and to rebuild the church and to found a monastery.

The Queen's devotion to the strangers naturally aroused interest. People came to listen to them and some stayed to be baptized. At last the King himself became a Christian and then his nobles followed their ruler's example.

When this news reached Pope Gregory, he sent another party of monks to England, including a young Italian named Paulinus. Their work was to help Augustine in spreading the Gospel in Kent and, across the Thames, among the East Saxons.

Augustine, now a bishop, made a long journey to meet the Welsh Christians at a place near the River Severn. Unfortunately, his proud manner offended the Welsh, who still held Devon, parts of Somerset and Wiltshire. There was a great Celtic church at Glastonbury and others at Llandaff, St Davids and Bangor. So the bishops of the old Christianity saw no reason why they should humbly accept Augustine as their archbishop. In any case, he had come from Kent, held by the hated Angles.

However, he was a man of God, even if they disagreed about such things as the date of Easter. If he rose to greet them, they would hear him meekly. But Augustine remained seated when the Welsh bishops arrived as if he were the teacher and they the pupils. So they said they would do none of the things he suggested nor would they have him as archbishop or help in converting the English.

The meeting was a failure and Augustine went back to continue his work in Kent, where he died and was buried in the new church of the monastery of Saints Peter and Paul at Canterbury.

QUEEN ETHELBURGA AND
ST PAULINUS

WHEN Queen Bertha died, the education of her little daughter, Ethelburga, was placed in the hands of Paulinus. The child and the tall young monk became close friends and they were rarely separated during the troubled days that lay ahead.

Pagan worship had not disappeared, even in Kent. Upon the death of King Ethelbert in 616, the priests of

the old religion persuaded his son, Edwald, to throw off
the Christian faith and to return to the pagan gods.
Most of the missionaries fled to Gaul, but not Paulinus or
Lawrence, the stout-hearted archbishop who had succeeded St Augustine.

Far from being frightened by the High Priest's
threats, Lawrence stormed into the King's Hall and
roundly accused young Edwald of betraying his parents'
noble memory. In a voice of thunder, he told how St
Peter himself had appeared in a dream to warn him of
the terrible things that would happen to the kingdom if

he and Paulinus were harmed. The King fell on his knees
in terror and begged Lawrence to take him back into
God's family.

Not long afterwards, a messenger arrived in Canterbury from the distant kingdom of Northumbria. He
had come, he said, to ask for the hand of Princess
Ethelburga for his master, King Edwin.

Edwald, now a good Christian, replied that he would
give his sister in marriage only if King Edwin promised
to allow her to keep her religion and to take her tutor
Paulinus with her.

The promise was given and the princess set out with a
strong bodyguard for the north of England. With her
travelled Paulinus and a helper named James the
Deacon.

The journey from one end of England to the other was
a long one and dangerous. The countryside was densely
wooded, the valleys were still undrained and likely to be
flooded in wet weather, and a vast area of marshes and
fens stretched south from the Wash.

Homeless men and robber-bands lurked in the woods
but her bodyguard and the names of two kings protected
Ethelburga. King Edwin's allies and vassals sent spear-
men to escort her to each vill or thane's hall at which she
rested after the day's travel.

At length she came to Northumbria and was nobly
welcomed by her royal lord, though he looked with
some suspicion at Paulinus and his companion James.

Edwin had led a hard, adventurous life. As a child his
father's kingdom had been taken and he had spent years
as a landless exile until he had won back his throne by
force of arms.

Older than Ethelburga, battle-scarred and wary,
Edwin took little interest in the religion of his beautiful
bride until he luckily escaped death from the knife of an

assassin sent by the King of the West Saxons. That same night, Queen Ethelburga gave birth to a daughter.

When Paulinus reminded Edwin of God's twofold mercy, the King was still cautious. He said that his baby daughter could be baptized in her mother's faith but, as for himself, he would only consider the matter if he was given victory over the West Saxons whom he was about to punish with fire and sword.

The Northumbrians duly defeated the enemy and Edwin, a man of his word, summoned Coifi, the High Priest, and all his nobles to a meeting at which Paulinus was to explain the Christian religion. Paulinus spoke with such fiery passion that all the warrior-nobles were silent. At length, an old thane rose to his feet.

'O King,' he said, 'the life of a man is like the flight of a sparrow through this Hall, as we sit at meat in winter with the fire blazing. It flies in from the darkness through one door into the warmth and light and out of the other, back to the darkness. Where it came from and where it goes we know not. Our life is as short as the flight of that sparrow. There are many things we do not know. If Paulinus can explain these things, we should follow his teaching.'

Then Coifi, the High Priest, sprang to his feet. Instead of defending the old gods, as everyone expected, he attacked them for their ingratitude. He had served them all his life and they had done nothing for him. Calling for a horse and a spear, he mounted and rode furiously to the temple where he hurled his weapon at the great wooden idol. Then he called upon the people to set fire to the unholy place.

After this, Edwin and all his Court were baptized. Then Paulinus and James the Deacon went out preaching throughout Northumbria. For five years, Edwin and Ethelburga ruled happily. They travelled about their kingdom, taking Paulinus with them and encouraging the people to become Christians. At York, the old Roman capital of the north, Edwin had begun to build a splendid church of stone when disaster struck the kingdom.

In 632 the forces of the Welsh King Cadwallon and Penda of Mercia came to attack the Northumbrians. They met at Hatfield Chase where the Northumbrian army was cut to pieces. Penda had Edwin's head carried into York on the point of a spear and his pagan troops harried the land.

Ethelburga and Paulinus were forced to flee and James the Deacon went into hiding. But they escaped to the coast where a ship carried them to Kent.

King Edwald was not strong enough to take vengeance upon the terrible Penda. All he could do to comfort his sister was to give her a royal estate at Lyminge where the Queen built a small minster, a double 'house', for nuns and monks, and here she ended her days as Abbess. Her friend Paulinus stayed with her for a time until he became Bishop of Rochester. It seemed as if their work in the north had been in vain.

HOW CHRISTIANITY SPREAD

BUT the light of Christianity had not failed. In secret places, James the Deacon preached to the faithful and taught them to sing. Then, a year after King Edwin's death, a new champion appeared. Oswald, a prince from another branch of the royal house, drove Penda out and became King of Northumbria.

Like King Edwin, Oswald had been a refugee. As a boy, he found shelter at Iona, where the monks baptized and educated him. Their kindness was fully repaid.

Having won his kingdom, Oswald sent to Iona for a priest to come and continue the work of Paulinus. The monk who came found the Northumbrians too stupid or obstinate for his liking and he returned in disgust to the island monastery. At this, his fellow-monks chose Aidan to take his place.

This humble, saintly man, working in perfect friendship with a generous king, transformed the kingdom of Northumbria. He built churches, trained boys for the priesthood and founded, on Lindisfarne, an island given him by Oswald, a monastery that was to become one of the most famous in the Western world.

Oswald, who once broke up a great silver dish and gave the pieces to the poor outside his thatched vill, did not reign long. The heathen Penda struck again and slew him, as he slew Sigbert, the Christian King of the East Angles.

Aidan and his monks clung to Lindisfarne, living like saints in their little community and braving the perils on the mainland. They carried on their work of converting the heathen, including even the Mercian invaders.

Another leader arose in King Oswy. He rallied the hardy Northumbrians and raised an army. At long last, Penda was defeated. In 655, at the battle of Winwood, the fierce old warrior, who had been a flail to Christians for more than thirty years, was killed. With Penda dead and his own son converted, Christianity could flourish in the Midlands and north of England.

Cuthbert, who, as a shepherd-boy, saw Aidan's soul carried to Heaven and who later served as a soldier against the heathen, carried God's message to the southern Picts. Loving and gentle to others, Cuthbert was stern to himself, for he went to live as a hermit on the Farne Island, so shut off from the world that he could see only the sky above the pit where he crouched alone.

There was a great respect for hermits and only after many doubts and prayers did the monks of Lindisfarne gently pull Cuthbert out of his cell to persuade him to be their bishop.

It was in Cuthbert's time that the Abbess Hilda, friend and kinswoman of King Oswy, founded the monastery at Whitby where Caedmon the cowherd received the gift of poetic song.

As Christianity took root and spread, there was one great question to be decided. Was England to be part of the Church of Western Europe under the rule of the Pope in Rome or was it to belong to the Celtic Church of Columba and Aidan?

The Celtic saints had performed the miracles of cour-

age and faith. They had carried the Word of God into Scotland and Northumbria at a time when Britain was cut off from the rest of the world. St Augustine had not been able to make friends with the Welsh bishops, but was friendship still impossible? The Celtic and the Roman Churches had several differences – the Celtic bishops, for instance, did not rule a definite district for they usually roamed about, preaching and baptizing – but the difference that troubled Christians most was that they held the solemn celebration of Easter on different dates.

In 633 King Oswy called a meeting, or synod, at Whitby. Abbot Wilfrid, who converted Sussex, Abbess Hilda, James the Deacon, still alive after all his adventures, bishops and clergy from all over Britain were there, including a priest from Kent who was chaplain to Ethelburga's daughter. After much discussion, they agreed to accept the Roman date for Easter.

Thus, the Church in Britain came under the authority of the Pope, although some of the clergy could not accept the change. Northern Ireland and Iona were slow to change, and in Wales they held to the old date for more than 100 years.

Five years after the Synod of Whitby, a great plague came into the land and carried off nearly all the clergy. To save the Church in Britain, the Pope chose as Archbishop of Canterbury a Greek monk from Tarsus in Asia Minor. His name was Theodore and for twenty-one years he laboured to bring order to the Church. He appointed bishops to take care of large districts in which they were to train priests for work in parishes. Theodore also founded new monasteries and encouraged the old ones to follow the Rule of St Benedict, the Italian saint whose monastery at Monte Cassino had been started in 529.

Theodore's work flowered into a golden age. English monasteries, English schools, English scholars and churchmen became famous throughout Europe. The Lindisfarne Gospel, with its wonderful illuminated capitals and covers of gold, the carved stone crosses, the new churches and the singing of the choirs in the great monasteries were the marvels of their time. The land was peaceful. There were quarrels between princes, of course, but the Welsh and the Picts were quiet and there was, as yet, no enemy from outside.

THE VENERABLE BEDE

IN the north-east a wise, kindly abbot brought up a boy named Bede. They lived at the joint monasteries of Wearmouth and Jarrow, whence the good abbot made the immense journey to Rome to fetch books for his brilliant pupil.

Working in his cell at Jarrow, the gentle Bede wrote book after book. The Scriptures, of course, were the scholar's chief subject but Bede interested himself in every branch of knowledge. He wrote about saints, stars, grammar, science, history and poetry. To him came pupils from all over Europe, though he himself never left his native Northumberland.

Bede's greatest work was his *History of the Church in England*, to which we owe most of our knowledge of the country's early history. At first he felt that he knew too little about events outside his own part of the country, but his friend Nothelm enlisted the help of churchmen in many places who sent facts and letters from which Bede fashioned his masterpiece.

He was a natural story-teller and no one has ever improved upon the beauty and simplicity of such tales as how Caedmon received the gift of song, how Cuthbert served God and how the old warrior likened the life of man to the flight of a sparrow.

This great work took many years and when it was finished, Bede was an old man. There were still books that must be written. He wished to translate the Gospel of St John from Latin into Anglo-Saxon, so that ordinary people could understand when it was read to them.

Knowing that time was short, Bede wrote on and on until he became too weak to hold a pen. A scribe wrote down his master's words. Bede urged him to hurry: 'Take thy pen and write quickly, for I have little time and after I'm gone, I do not want my boys to read what is untrue.'

The scribe went on until it was almost dark in the cell. 'There is just one more sentence to write, dear master,' he said.

Bede gathered his strength and spoke, 'Then write quickly, my son.'

Presently the monk sighed happily, 'It is finished, master.'

'Thou hast spoken truly,' murmured the old man. 'All is finished.'

He died during the night, having continued to the end his work for God. This was the spirit of good men everywhere. A man had a gift; it might be for writing or carving or building or merely for tending the sheep – whatever the gift, he used it for the glory of God.

ENGLISH CHURCHMEN ABROAD

SOME men, like Bede, stayed at home to carry out their work. Others went abroad at this time to take into northern Europe the faith and learning that had come to England from over the sea.

The Saxon tribes of Germany were still heathens and to them went men like Wilfrid of York and Willibrod of Northumbria. The greatest of the English missionaries was St Boniface, son of a Wessex landowner, who spent his life converting the fierce tribesmen and was murdered at his task in the bleak coastland of Frisia.

Thus, when Charlemagne, the mighty ruler of Frankland, wanted to establish learning in his dominions, he naturally turned to the land that produced so many notable scholars and churchmen.

In Italy, the King of the Franks chanced to meet an Englishman journeying home from Rome with books and with the 'pallium', a special robe, for his archbishop. When Charlemagne learned that the traveller was none other than Alcuin of York, the most famous scholar of the day, he could not rest until he won consent from his king and archbishop to have him at his own court.

So, for the rest of his life, the cheerful, hard-working Alcuin acted as chief adviser to Charlemagne. He joined his travelling court and later founded the palace school at Aachen, and another famous school at Tours, where Alcuin ended his life as Abbot in 804.

Between them the English monk and the jovial, masterful emperor established abbeys and schools that lasted far longer than Charlemagne's conquests.

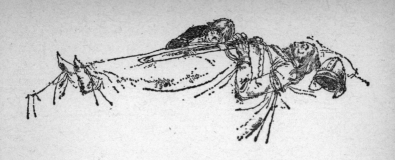

THE ENGLISH KINGDOMS

ALTHOUGH the Church was now united, England was still divided into a number of kingdoms that rose and fell, according to the character and strength of their rulers.

Life was short. Only rarely did a man live as long as Penda and Charlemagne. Most men, including kings, died before they were forty and since the dead king's sons were usually boys and since there was no fixed rule about an eldest son succeeding his father, the death of a king was usually a disaster for the realm. His brothers, his wife's relatives and the great nobles usually fought and schemed for power until one came to the top and brought some kind of order to the land.

In the seventh century, the greatest kingdom was Northumbria. The influence of Iona, the work of saintly abbots and good kings brought strength and unity to the north-east. But, during the eighth century, there was a succession of short-lived kings who could not check the rise of Mercia.

This midland kingdom had only two rulers in eighty years. Aethelbald, a warrior and something of a tyrant who was told to mend his ways by the courageous Boniface, extended his rule as far as London. All the

Anglo-Saxon kings south of the Humber acknowledged
him as their overlord until, in 757, Aethelbald was murdered by one of his own bodyguard. This led to a short
period of civil war until Offa, a relative of the dead man,
made himself undisputed king.

Although much of his career is wrapped in legend we
know that Offa was strong enough to be called 'the
Great', and to give himself the title of 'King of the English'. Even the mighty Charlemagne regarded Offa as
almost an equal, made a trade treaty with him, sent gifts
and considered joining their two families by marriage.
When a quarrel occurred, perhaps over the marriage
arrangements, Charlemagne thought about invasion
but, instead, he sent his friend Alcuin to patch up the
friendship.

Offa was certainly powerful enough to receive am-
bassadors from the Pope, to mint his own coins and to
crush the sub-kingdom of Kent. To defend Mercia from
the Welsh, he built a huge earthwork, known as Offa's
Dyke, from Cheshire to the Bristol Channel and, in this
orderly kingdom, he founded many churches and monasteries, among them the Abbey at St Albans which was
built in honour of the first British martyr.

When Offa's long reign came to an end in 796, the
usual troubles broke out. His son reigned only five
months and was followed by a distant cousin. Kent and
Wessex rebelled and Mercia began to decline. It was
still a kingdom to reckon with, but it was no longer
supreme.

The star of Wessex was rising. This southern kingdom
had been growing in strength since about 700, when one
of its kings, Ine of Wessex, had the laws of his realm
written down, an unusual thing to do in days when justice was based on custom known to all men.

In 802 Egbert, son of one of Offa's enemies, became

King of Wessex. He defeated the Mercians and made Wessex into the strongest of the English kingdoms. By a hairsbreadth, it was to prove strong enough to save Christianity from the heathens.

THE COMING OF THE NORTHMEN

OUT of the northern seas, from the fiords of Norway and from the windswept islands where Boniface was killed, came a horde of robbers more terrible than the barbarians who had once captured Rome.

They were called Norsemen, Danes, Vikings, Northmen or, simply, 'the heathen host', and everywhere they appeared they struck terror by their pitiless greed and blood-lust.

In their horned helmets, carrying bright spears and two-handed axes, the sea-pirates gloried in slaughter as they gloried in their jewelled arm-bands and scarlet cloaks. They would kill in a kind of frenzied joy, and what they could not carry off in the way of loot they smashed and hurled into the flames. Spreading terror was part of the raiders' business. People gave them gold to go away and they came back for more in the spring, when the raiding season opened.

The first warning came in 787. A monk wrote in the
Anglo-Saxon Chronicle:

'In this year, the King [of Wessex] took to wife the
daughter of Offa. And in his days, came three ships
and the Reeve rode thither and tried to compel them
to go to the royal manor, for he did not know who they
were and then they slew him. These were the first
ships of the Danes to come to England.'

Six years after the murder of the King's Reeve, a fleet
appeared off the holy island of Lindisfarne, where the
Northmen went ashore to rip down the hangings of Cuthbert's church, to seize the vessels of gold and silver and
to break the skulls of the helpless monks. Next year
Bede's monastery at Jarrow was receiving the same
treatment when a force of Northumbrians came up in
time to interrupt the looting and drive off the robbers.

After this no abbey or headland or river bank was
safe. Not even Charlemagne could stop the raids along
his coasts. The grey sea was wide and no one knew where
the Northmen would strike next. Sailing their long
dragon-ships with magnificent skill, they came to unpro-
tected shores, entered the river mouths and spread across
the land on stolen horses. Villages and monasteries were
sacked with merciless greed. Then, when they had thrust
the bright cloth, the crosses and altar cups into the bows
of their ships alongside their terrified captives, they
sailed away.

Some of the Northmen went down the rivers into
Russia, some along the Frankish coast and into the
Mediterranean as far as Constantinople. Others crossed
the sea to Scotland and the Shetlands, Orkneys and
Hebrides felt their fury; Iona itself was sacked in 802
and the robbers went on to Ireland. Here, as in Scotland

and the Isle of Man, they took land and founded kingdoms with fortified towns from which they could launch
fresh raids.

There were Northmen who sailed as far as Iceland
and Greenland. Some, it is said, even reached America
which they called Vinland, because of the wild grapes
they found growing in some sheltered spot. But far easier
and far more profitable was the voyage across the North
Sea. They called it the Swan's Road and it led to
England.

Naturally, the east coast suffered first and longest.
Then, as plunder became scarce, the dragon-ships sailed
through the Channel to attack the southern coasts.

No sooner had King Egbert beaten the Mercians than
his own kingdom was in danger. In 835 he was fighting
'a pirate host' in Cornwall and, after his death a year
later, his son Ethelwulf was having to fend off the enemy
all along the coast from Dorset to the Thames.

By this time the roofless abbeys and the blackened
monastery walls could yield no more treasures, so the
Vikings came, not in private groups of two or three
ships, but in great fleets. They came to settle a land that
was fairer than their own and, when they had taken
farms, they showed as much skill with the plough as they
had shown with sword and axe.

In the year 851 a fleet of 350 longships sailed into the
mouth of the Thames. An army went ashore to storm

London and Canterbury. The Mercians were defeated and Surrey was overrun. Then Ethelwulf and the West Saxons marched up from Winchester and gave the Danes the worst beating they had ever suffered.

ALFRED THE GREAT

SO great was King Ethelwulf's victory that he felt able to go on a visit to Rome that lasted a year. He took with him his little son, Alfred, for he had left the kingdom in the hands of the boy's older brothers.

On their return, the travellers found that the Danes were stronger than ever, for defeat in the south had merely caused them to turn their attention to the midlands and the north.

Before he died, in 855, Ethelwulf directed that the older part of Wessex should go to his son Ethelbald and the eastern part (Kent, Sussex, Surrey and Essex) to Ethelbert. This division of the kingdom seemed to bring a curse upon the House of Wessex, for one disaster followed another.

Ethelbald died after a reign of five years. Ethelbert, who joined the kingdom together again, had just beaten off the host that captured Winchester, his capital, when he too died. Aethelred, the third of the royal brothers, became King as the Danes mounted their largest attack so far.

News reached Wessex that a 'Great Army' had taken York with horrid slaughter. The whole of Northumbria, with all its store of art and learning, had fallen into the bloodstained grip of the heathens.

The King of Mercia was too terrified to fight. Aethelred led the men of Wessex up to Nottingham to offer support but the Mercians made peace. So the Wessex fyrd, or army, went glumly back to their homes. But young Alfred had seen the terrible Northmen and had

noted their habit of building camps so strong that it was well-nigh impossible to dislodge them. From these fortified camps they could raid in any direction they pleased and, if they met with a reverse, they had a stronghold to fall back upon that was filled with captured stores, enough to last the winter, if need be.

In 870 the Northmen sprang at East Anglia, killed King Edmund in battle and took his entire kingdom. Then they turned towards Wessex.

The host marched to Reading in the valley of the Thames and here King Aethelred attacked their stockade. Failing to take it, he retreated into open country. The Danes followed and made a surprise attack at Ashdown when the King was still at his prayers. Alfred, however, 'fighting like a wild boar', beat the enemy off with heavy losses.

Once again, defeat did not weaken the Danes. They loved fighting and went off to spend a year ravaging the eastern part of Mercia. After that, they were ready to try another assault on Wessex.

In 871 attacks were made by land and sea. Aethelred died at Easter and Alfred, hastily elected King by the

Witan, fought in nine battles that summer. His forces were exhausted but so was the enemy. The Danes withdrew into Mercia and Alfred took stock of the situation.

He was only twenty-two and, although he was by no means robust, he had been fighting since he was old enough to carry a spear. The only peace Alfred had ever known was during his childhood, when he had learnt to read at his mother's knee while his brothers scornfully played war-games. There had been a little schooling from the monks and the long-remembered visit to Rome.

But now there was no time for the things he really loved. He must fight for what was left of his battered kingdom.

As Alfred and every thane and cottager expected, the Northmen came back. Under a resolute leader, Guthrum, their main army drove deep into Dorset; another force moved in from the west and a great fleet appeared off the south coast. Exeter was captured but Alfred was still clinging on to the fringe of the invading host when a storm wrecked the enemy fleet and strewed the shore with the bodies of thousands of Danes.

Guthrum retreated to Gloucester and the people of Wessex breathed again. Winter was coming on and the foe would quit warfare until the spring. At least, there were a few beasts left for the feasts at Christmastide.

Guthrum watched and waited. At Twelfth Night, when the season of feasting reached its height, he struck across the frozen land and took Chippenham by storm. Making this his main camp, he harried the countryside with ferocious speed.

Caught by surprise, the fighting-men of Wessex were swept aside. Their leaders were scattered or slain. The kingdom lay broken as the pagan horde swept across the land.

THE VALIANT KING

ALFRED escaped. With his family and most of his own bodyguard he fled to the Somerset marshes, where only the swamp-men knew the paths that led through shoulder-tall reeds to a patch of solid ground called Athelney. Here, Alfred built a stronghold from which he sent messengers to his friends and spies to watch the enemy.

The tale of the lonely fugitive being scolded by a cottage wife for allowing her cakes to burn was written long after Alfred's death. It may be true, but at least he was not alone. Saxons came through the Sedgemoor marsh to join him; raiding parties went out to give the Northmen a taste of their own brew and one of these bands took the enemy by surprise and captured his Raven Banner.

Spirits rose high at Athelney. A spy came in (some said that it was Alfred himself) to tell how he had got into Guthrum's camp disguised as a harper. He had seen with his own eyes the Danes feasting day after day, using up their stores because they believed that Wessex was finished.

But Wessex was awake and ready to strike back.

Alfred left Athelney and made his way, like the thousands he had summoned, to the meeting-place at Egbert's Stone, high upon the Wiltshire downs. There the men of Wessex shouted and wept to see their valiant King alive and in their midst again.

The Danes came out of camp to face the Saxons at Ethandune, fifteen miles from Chippenham. With the deep-throated roar of men who remembered their blackened farmsteads and slaughtered children, the West Saxons burst the Danish ranks and swept their hated foes into headlong flight. They did not pause to celebrate the victory but drove hard after the enemy until the survivors were securely imprisoned in the Chippenham fortress.

Alfred tightened his grip. For once it was the Saxons who had food and fire, but, within the stockade, the Danish stores had gone and the wounded died of hunger and cold. At last, after two weeks, Guthrum surrendered.

The time of vengeance had come. For more than a lifetime the Danes had killed and robbed without pity and now a Danish army was to meet its doom. The West

Saxons looked at the prisoners and ran their thumbs along the sharpened edges of axes and spears.

But there was no massacre. Alfred gave the order not to kill but to feed his foes. In victory he showed the nobility of greatness.

Awed by such mercy, Guthrum made peace. He agreed to withdraw his army from Wessex for ever and he consented to be baptized into the Christian faith.

The Peace of Wedmore saved Wessex. Eight years later, Alfred was strong enough to occupy London and to rebuild its broken walls. He had to teach the Danes another lesson or two and, thenceforward, they were made to keep to the Danelaw, the land lying east of a line from Chester to Essex. They settled to farming and trade but Alfred could never relax. He knew that many of the jarls, or earls, were not bound by the peace that he had made with Guthrum and there were others across the sea still hoping to find land and plunder.

To hold what he had saved, Alfred built a fleet that could tackle the enemy on the sea. The walls of London would repel an invader and, in Wessex itself, forts were

built and towns made strong with earth banks and wooden palisades. To prevent the kingdom being caught defenceless again, Alfred divided the fyrd into two parts, one to tend the fields and the other, in its turn, to stand to arms.

But Alfred was not called 'the Great' simply because he was a good general. At heart, he was a man of peace and, in those dire months at Athelney, he had come to realize what his people needed.

Wessex was well-nigh ruined. Trade had ceased, the farms were derelict, the churches and monasteries were roofless and empty. The people were hungry and lawless.

Almost single-handed, Alfred rebuilt the kingdom. He travelled up and down the land, praising and encouraging, building with his own hands, learning crafts and setting others to work. He fetched skilled men from abroad to teach the Saxons the arts they had forgotten, for on every side he found ignorance:

'Hardly a man in the kingdom can read his prayer-book or write a letter,' he said. 'I would have all the boys now in England set to learning.'

Schools were started and even the nobles had to go to their lessons if they wished to receive the King's favour:

'It was a strange sight,' wrote a bishop, 'to see eldermen and officials, ignorant from boyhood, learning to read.'

Since few teachers were left alive, invitations were sent to France, Wales and Ireland for monks and scholars to come and work in Wessex. Not all of them were good men and, to Alfred's sorrow, they sometimes quarrelled. Once, two of the foreign monks actually killed their abbot. But among the newcomers was a Welsh monk named Asser, who became Alfred's greatest friend and helper.

Books had almost completely disappeared, so Alfred kept the scribes at their desks making copies of old books that had escaped the flames. Almost all were written in Latin, for there had been little or no writing in Anglo-Saxon since Bede's time. Alfred set himself to improve his own knowledge of Latin, and, with Asser's help, he translated parts of the Bible and works on history, geography and science.

This wonderful man never ceased toiling for his people. He found time for building, writing and governing and was keenly interested in stars, in trade and in foreign places. He re-wrote the laws of King Ine and kept in touch with the Pope, for it was his Christian faith that gave him the strength to do so much. As one of the monks wrote:

'The King attends daily services of religion . . . he goes to church at night-time to pray secretly, unknown to anyone.'

The noblest man who ever occupied an English throne died when he was barely fifty, but he left an example to his people and a message to his successors:

'I pray thee, my good son, be a father to my people,' he said as he lay dying. 'Comfort the poor, protect and shelter the weak and put right the things that are wrong.'

THE SONS OF ALFRED

AT his death, Alfred's kingdom was not England, but Wessex, the southern part. Even so, his victory over the invader had placed Wessex far above the other kingdoms and they never rose again. There were to be no more independent kings of Mercia, Northumbria and East Anglia. It was Alfred's family that would supply the true kings of England.

Edward the Elder, Alfred's son, who reigned until 924, spent all his life fighting the Danes to extend his father's boundaries. He was a splendid soldier and his companion-in-arms was his sister, Ethelfleda, Alfred's eldest child.

At sixteen, Ethelfleda had married a war-scarred Mercian nobleman named Aethelred. This marriage linked the two kingdoms in friendship, although much of Mercia had been lost to the Danes. With a puppet-king in the enemy's power, Mercians looked on Aethelred as their leader and, for several years, his wife rode to war at his side and, when he died, she took over leadership of the army.

Known as 'The Lady of the Mercians', Alfred's daughter worked in perfect harmony with her brother when he became King of Wessex. Indeed, she brought up his son, Athelstan, a handsome boy who grew into a great general through assisting his dauntless aunt in her campaigns.

Edward the Elder and Ethelfleda developed a new way of fighting the Danes. After she had defeated the Welsh and made her border strong against attack by those tribesmen, Ethelfleda harassed the Danes along Watling Street, while her brother attacked them in the midlands. As they advanced, they built forts called burghs, so that they could not easily be dislodged from the territory that they were steadily winning.

These tactics succeeded. The Danes were still strong but they had no leader like Guthrum to unite them. Instead, they fought under a number of chiefs, called jarls or earls, whom Ethelfleda defeated one by one, while Edward pressed into East Anglia and won a great victory near Huntingdon.

Derby was taken by storm, Leicester surrendered and the Danes of York had agreed to yield to the Lady of the Mercians when she died at a fort on Watling Street in 919.

By the time Athelstan succeeded his father, the Danes had been pushed so far back that he was able to advance north of the Humber into what had been the kingdom of Northumbria. Here the Norwegians (who had settled along the coasts of Ireland and western Scotland) were in command but, in 937, Athelstan won a great victory at a place called Brunanburgh.

We do not know where Brunanburgh was but the writer of the *Anglo-Saxon Chronicle* was so moved by the victory that he turned to poetry to describe it:

> 'In this year, Athelstan, Lord of the warriors,
>   with his brother, Prince Edmund,

Won undying glory with the edges of swords
In warfare round Brunanburgh.
With their hammered blades, the sons of Edward
Clove the shield-wall. . . .
                              There lay many a warrior
Of the men of the North, torn by spears,
Shot o'er his shield: likewise many a Scot,
Sated with battle, lay lifeless.
All through the day, the West Saxons in troops
Pressed on in pursuit of the hostile peoples
Fiercely, with swords sharpened on grindstones,
They cut down the fugitives as they fled.'

After this battle, Athelstan could truly claim to be
King of England, for he ruled, or was overlord, from the
Isle of Wight to the River Clyde in Scotland. But, as
long as the Danes submitted, he left them to live their
lives and to follow their own customs.

When the great Athelstan died in 941, it seemed as if
the new-found strength of the kingdom might ebb away.
Three kings followed each other in quick succession.
They were Edmund, stabbed by an outlaw, Edred, his
warrior-brother, and Edwig, who ruled badly and drove
St Dunstan, then a bishop, out of the kingdom.

Fortunately, Edwig's reign was short and Edgar, who
became King in 959, when he was only sixteen, ruled the
kingdom so well that he was called Edgar the Peace-
able.

An old story tells how Edgar, to show his mastery of
the whole islands, had himself rowed in a boat on the
River Dee by a crew of six 'kings'. At all events, his reign
was quiet enough for him to be able to follow his passion
for building monasteries.

When Dunstan had fled abroad, he had stayed at a
monastery in Flanders where he found monks living far

more strictly than the easy-going English. This impressed him and, on his return, when he was Archbishop of Canterbury, Dunstan set to work to reform monastic life in his own country. With the enthusiastic help of King Edgar and two bishops, new Benedictine monasteries were built on land given cheerfully by the King and less willingly by the nobles. Lazy and sinful monks were turned out of the old abbeys and there was a revival of learning in the Church.

Under a good King and a great Archbishop, Anglo-Saxon England was rich and peaceful, except in the ravaged north. The King was only thirty-two and there seemed to be a long period of prosperity ahead, when Edgar died suddenly in 975. At once the kingdom fell into evil hands.

ETHELRED THE UNREADY

BY his first marriage Edgar had a son named Edward, and then he married a widow, Elfrith, who bore him a second son, Ethelred. Neither boy was old enough to rule and a struggle took place between the supporters of the elder son and the powerful friends of the Queen who wanted to see her son upon the throne.

The Witan chose Edward but, in 978, when on a visit to his stepmother, at Corfe in Dorset, the young King was treacherously murdered and hastily buried without so much as a church service. Men dared not say that the Queen had planned this crime but no one was punished for it and her son Ethelred became King, as she had hoped.

At a later date the murdered boy, known as Edward the Martyr, was buried at Shaftesbury where miracles were said to have occurred at his tomb.

Thus, hoisted to the throne by murder, Ethelred's reign began badly. As he grew older, it was clear that he had none of the qualities of his great ancestors. He was not brave or skilled in arms; owing, perhaps, to the events of his childhood, he had no trust in himself or in others. With his evil mother forever at his elbow, he presided weakly over a quarrelsome Court, where nobles betrayed each other and plotted to recover the Church lands that they had been made to give away in Edgar's time.

The name Ethelred meant 'noble counsel' but it was not long before men added the bitter nickname, 'Unraed', meaning 'no counsel'. Ethelred the Unraed was 'Noble Counsel – No Counsel' or, in modern speech, 'the Unready'. But, apart from the King, the whole country was unready for the disasters that were about to fall upon it. New packs of sea-wolves came out from the Danish islands, where training-camps had been set up to teach young warriors the secrets of successful raiding.

The first of the new-style raids occurred at Southampton in 984 when most of the inhabitants were killed or captured. Thanet and Dorset were the next to suffer and, in 991, Olaf Tryggvason came to Folkestone with ninety-three ships, burnt all the countryside and the town of Sandwich, crossed into Essex, captured Ipswich and defeated the Saxon army at Maldon.

The raids grew worse when Olaf was joined by Sweyn Forkbeard, the ferocious son of the King of Denmark. They captured London in 994 and did tremendous damage. King Ethelred, instead of calling every man in the realm to arms, feebly invited the Danes to Andover where he had Olaf baptized and made him a gift of gold.

From that time on, Ethelred's only plan was to buy off the Danes. A heavy tax called the Danegeld was laid on the people. The invaders came killing and robbing; then they were given money to stop. They took it, laughing, and went away. Soon they were back for more.

Yet what could Ethelred do? He was no soldier himself and his nobles were treacherous. They failed to protect each other's land and sometimes, when it suited them, they actually joined the robbers. In the south, the leaderless people had no heart to fight, and in the old Danelaw the inhabitants were not likely to oppose their own kinsfolk.

In his difficulty, Ethelred gave land in southern England to certain Danes on condition that they would fight

for him. Among them was the jarl Pallig who was married to Gunnhilda, sister of Sweyn Forkbeard.

In 1002 the Vikings harried Devonshire and all the country as far as Southampton. Pallig, who should have come to help the King's forces, did not appear and the King and the Witan were forced to find another huge sum to buy off the victors.

Ethelred was furious. In his rage, he gave secret orders that every Dane living in England was to be killed on November 13th, St Brice's Day.

The massacre took place and among the slaughtered were Pallig and Gunnhilda. When Forkbeard heard this news he swore a great oath to avenge his sister's murder.

For ten years the Danes raked the land with fire and death. Each summer they harried the countryside, and in winter they retired to the Isle of Wight or to their favourite base at Reading. Some returned to Denmark and came back in the spring with fresh recruits for the marauding host.

By 1013, when Sweyn and his eighteen-year-old son, Canute, landed with yet another army, the stricken people were sick of pillage and slaughter. To put an end to their sufferings, they offered to take Sweyn as their King. Ethelred the Unready fled to his brother-in-law in Normandy.

But Sweyn was never crowned. He died suddenly in London and young Canute, uncertain what to do, went back to Denmark to seek advice from his older brother.

EDMUND IRONSIDE

AT once Ethelred returned. He was full of promises to rule well and he brought with him his son, Edmund, a young giant, full of courage and determination. While Prince Edmund put his heart into rallying his countrymen, Ethelred and Edric, his boon-companion, were busy taking revenge on those who had accepted the Dane for King.

This Edric was a Mercian earl, so renowned for his greed that he had earned the name of Edric the Grasper. With a force of his own picked ruffians, he was seizing land and riches when Canute appeared in East Anglia with a strong army.

Prince Edmund naturally expected that Edric would bring his Mercians to join the Men of Wessex. But the Grasper was jealous of the valiant prince and he marched away to offer his services to the Dane.

Edmund was forced to retreat, as all the north and the midlands surrendered. He fell back to London and here his father died. The stout-hearted Londoners, who had known many a siege, acclaimed Edmund as their King and manned the walls as Canute drew near.

The King slipped away, for his last hope lay in Alfred's country. The farmers of Wessex were still the best fighting-men in England and they flocked to Edmund's standard.

As in Alfred's day, they were equal to the best of the Danes when their own King was in the thick of the fight, swinging his war-axe and roaring the old battle-cry. They fought the enemy, drove him back, closed in and fought him again. Edmund's prowess at this time earned him the name of Edmund Ironside.

There was a battle that lasted for two days in Wiltshire, where Edric the Grasper, serving with the Danes, tried to snatch victory by a trick. Hacking off the head of a fallen man, he held it up, crying, 'See, the head of your King! Fly, Saxons, fly!'

But Edmund tore off his helmet to show his face, 'I live! I live!' he shouted. 'Edmund is here!' The enraged Saxons tried to reach the traitor but, although they broke the Danish ranks, Edric escaped from the field.

Canute fell back and Edmund was able to relieve London. He cleared Kent of the Danes and chased them across the Thames into Essex. His army was drawn up opposite the foe when the Grasper himself came into Edmund's camp and offered to do homage if he could serve on the Saxon side.

Edmund hesitated. The earl was a traitor but his Mercian soldiers would make victory certain. Edmund gave his hand to Edric and placed him on his army's right wing. At this, Canute decided to retreat to his ships for he knew that he was outnumbered.

Seeing his chance, Edmund gave the order to charge but, at the crucial moment, Edric played him false. He wheeled his men about and took no part in the fight, so that Canute recovered and was able to drive back the dismayed Saxons.

Once more Edmund retreated to the west and Canute followed cautiously. But, in Gloucestershire, instead of offering battle, he asked for a truce. The two leaders met on an island in the River Severn and agreed that peace was better than war between men so well matched in valour. Canute was to rule in the north and the east; Edmund would rule in the south. When one died, the other would have all.

Within a year, Edmund Ironside was dead. No one knew how he died. Some said it was a sudden illness, but others whispered that Edric had poisoned him to win Canute's favour. If he did, it was in vain, for the Dane put him to death for his crimes.

CANUTE THE SEA KING

SWEARING to rule by the laws of Alfred and Edgar,
Canute was crowned King of England in the year 1016.
He was a remarkable man, this Viking who had first
come as a robber but had stayed to be King. Moreover,
he was to rule as well as the best of those who followed
Alfred.

First, Canute made sure of his throne by banishing
Edmund's little sons to distant Hungary. Then he

married King Ethelred's widow, Emma of Normandy, and he recruited a bodyguard of housecarls to guard him night and day. Having thus made sure that he would not be removed by rivals or by an assassin's knife, Canute gave the people order and justice. He allowed Saxons and Danes to live according to their own customs and he refused to favour one race more than the other.

Born a heathen, Canute became a Christian and did his best to make amends for all the damage done to the church. He went on a pilgrimage to Rome and, in England, he built monasteries, including one at Bury St Edmunds in honour of the East Anglian king slain by the Danes. At Canterbury, he had a rich shrine made for the bones of St Alphage, the archbishop whom the Danes captured in 1012 and killed during a drunken feast when they hurled their meat-bones at their captive until he died.

Soon after he became King of England, Canute succeeded his brother as King of Denmark and, later, in 1028, he seized the throne of Norway, with dominion over Greenland, the Scottish Isles and the Isle of Man. Thus, he was master of three kingdoms, of the North Sea and the Baltic. This may explain the story of courtiers flattering him by saying that he commanded the ocean, whereupon he proved their folly by placing his chair at the edge of the sea and vainly ordering the waves to go back. Had Canute lived longer, England might have become part of a Scandinavian sea-empire, but he died in 1035 and was buried beside the Saxon kings at Winchester.

His younger son, Hardicanute, was fighting in Norway when his father died, so his stepbrother, Harold Harefoot, became King of England without opposition. Within two years he was dead and Hardicanute took the crown. He must have been a worthless man and a drunkard, for the chronicler wrote of him, 'he never did anything worthy of a king while he reigned and he died as he stood at his drink at Lambeth.'

In 1042 the Witan chose the king of the 'rightful' line, for they elected Edward, the forty-year-old son of Ethelred the Unready and Emma of Normandy.

EDWARD THE CONFESSOR

AS a boy, Edward had been taken for safety to his mother's land, where he was brought up at the court of his uncle, Duke Richard. The delicate, timid lad came to think of himself as a Norman; he had Norman tastes and Norman friends, he spoke Norman-French and he felt that he was a stranger in England.

The Normans had come from the same creeks as the sea-robbers who had attacked King Alfred's realm. Their great-grandfathers had ravaged the coasts of France, until one of them named Rollo had been given or had taken the province that came to be called Normandy.

Their Viking energy went into farming and horse-rearing, into fighting the dukes of France and, presently, into church-building. The Normans took up Christianity with enthusiasm and soon became famous for their splendid churches and for the strict lives of their monks and clergy.

It was this side of the Norman character that Edward inherited. Where most high-born knights had an appetite for battle and wealth, he had a passion for religion. It was not that he was particularly kind and good, but he loved churches, ceremonies, prayers and holy relics, such as the bones of saints and those scraps of wood and cloth that were supposed to have some marvellous power.

Despite his reputation for holiness, Edward was not popular in England. The greatest man in the kingdom was Earl Godwin of Essex, who meant to be the power behind a weakling's throne. But, although Godwin managed to marry his daughter Edith to the King, he and his sons were cold-shouldered at court.

Edward brought some of his Norman friends and priests with him. Others came to join them and it was not long before they were hated for the arrogant contempt with which they treated the Queen and her countrymen.

One day, the Count of Bologne, who had been visiting the King and was on his way to his ships, rode into Dover with his men and demanded food and lodging from the local householders. A townsman lost his temper when spoken to like a dog; blows were struck and, in the brawl, the men of Dover killed several of the visitors.

King Edward summoned Earl Godwin, whose lands stretched from Dorset to Kent, and angrily ordered him to burn Dover as a punishment. Godwin refused, declaring that the upstarts had only got what they deserved. For this disobedience he and his turbulent sons were banished from the realm.

Queen Edith was sent to a nunnery and Edward, greatly pleased with himself, invited his Norman friends to help themselves to Earl Godwin's lands.

Among the visitors from Normandy was Edward's cousin, the grim young Duke William. He looked around and liked all that he saw. It was a brief visit but, before he departed, he obtained from his childless cousin a promise that he should one day have the crown of England. If William had made enquiries, he would have discovered that the promise was worthless, for the crown went to the man chosen by the Witan.

Earl Godwin was known to be a hard, ambitious man but the English were in no mood to have their own countrymen exiled for a pack of foreigners. It was not long, therefore, before the Earl deemed it safe to return from Flanders and his son, Harold, came with a fleet from Ireland. Together, their forces were too much for the timid King who agreed to restore their lands, to recall Queen Edith and to send his Norman friends away.

Godwin did not enjoy his triumph long. He died within a few months and his titles and most of his lands fell to Harold, who became the real ruler of the kingdom.

As time went on, the King became known as Edward the Confessor. He was content to leave earthly affairs to the able young nobleman, for his own thoughts were fixed on Heaven and on the great abbey that he was building at Westminster.

Harold ruled well. Short but immensely strong, he had energy, good looks and a leader's power to make men love him. When Griffith, King of Gwynedd (North Wales), made an alliance with the treacherous Earl of Mercia, Harold crushed the rebellion with impressive skill. His fame grew, for he was as generous and fair-minded as he was brave. It was clear that he would have

justice in the realm and he sternly warned his unruly brother Tostig, Earl of Northumbria, that he must mend his ways and give better government to the people in the north.

But, for all his talents, Harold was a luckless man. In 1065 he was sailing in the Channel on the King's business when a storm wrecked his ship on the coast of France. Captured by the surly Count of Ponthieu, he was handed over to Duke William of Normandy.

His rival concealed his glee and entertained the Englishmen with lavish hospitality, but he would not let them go home.

At length, desperate to get away, Harold fell into a trap. He agreed to swear an oath that he would support Duke William's claim to the English crown. In his heart, he meant to break his word, for a man could not be held to a forced oath. But William understood his rival's thoughts. After the oath was made, a cloth was removed from the chest on which Harold had laid his hand and, to the horror of the Englishmen, it was seen that the chest was filled with holy bones. It was no ordinary oath

that had been sworn and, in the future, Harold would be called oath-breaker and his men's hearts would be filled with dread.

Back in England, Harold had to deal with a rebellion in the north caused by his brother's misdeeds. Showing no favour to his own family, he sent Tostig into exile, an act of justice that was to cost him his throne and his life.

Meanwhile, King Edward was dying. Too ill to attend the opening of Westminster Abbey, he died in January 1066 and was buried in his great church. The Witan met in London and chose Harold to be King of England. The claims of Edmund Ironside's grandson, of the King of Norway and of Duke William were not even considered.

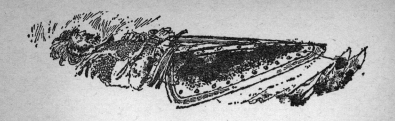

HAROLD, LAST OF THE SAXONS

WHEN William of Normandy heard the news, he broke into a rage and proclaimed a crusade to win his 'rights'. While an invasion fleet was being built, hundreds of knights rode in to join his army, attracted like flies to honey by the thoughts of plunder and land. The Pope himself sent his blessing and a banner, for William had made his tale good, although his claim to England was no more than an excuse for a military adventure.

Harold did not fear the Normans. Indeed, he longed for them to come all through the summer of 1066, for he had a splendid army assembled in the southern counties, far stronger than any sea-borne force that William might bring. He was as good a soldier as the Duke, though more hot-headed, and he had an excellent fleet that would have given the Norman ships a rough passage in the Channel.

The summer wore on and the Normans still did not come, for the wind blew steadily from the north and kept their ships from sailing. As the corn grew ripe, the English soldiers became restive, thinking of their farms and harvest-time. Surely the Normans would not come so late to risk the autumn storms and a winter campaign?

Harold had just disbanded his army and sent the fleet

to the Thames, when a call for help came from the north. Three hundred longships had sailed into the Humber and an army of Norsemen, led by Harold Hardrada, King of Norway, was ravaging the land like a pack of wolves. Earl Tostig was there with the invaders, for he had invited Harold Hardrada, the giant Viking who had fought all over Europe, to come to take his brother's throne.

Hardrada defeated the Earls of Mercia and Northumbria, and made them promise to help him against Harold. Then they waited for the English King at Stamford Bridge, a wooden bridge that crossed the Derwent, seven miles from York.

With housecarls and as many fighting-men as he could gather, Harold came north at furious speed. In York, he learned that the enemy was only a short distance off, so, refusing to rest, he drove his tired men on without a pause. They came to Stamford Bridge, where the Norwegian host was camped on both banks, their armour laid aside and their ranks unformed.

Harold sent a message to Tostig. He would pardon him and restore his earldom if he came across to the English side.

'And what land will my brother give to Harold Hardrada?'

Angrily, Harold replied, 'To the King of Norway, I will give six feet of English earth. No, seven feet, seeing that he is taller than other men and needs a longer grave!'

Then he gave the order to attack. The English broke through the forces on the west bank of the river but were checked by a gigantic Viking who held the bridge until he was speared from below by a soldier who had crept under the timbers. Once across the river, the English infantry cut the host to pieces and, as Harold Hardrada and Tostig lay dead on the field, they chased the remnant back to the ships.

Harold had kept his word. The most famous war-captain lay in his seven-foot grave, the pirate army was destroyed and only a few survivors were sailing ruefully back to Norway. The English buried their dead and tended the wounded, as the monks sang the Thanksgiving in York Minster.

But the wind that carried the Norwegians away brought the Normans to the coast of Sussex, where William landed his army without so much as a fishing-boat or a ploughboy to oppose him. Like all great commanders, William made the most of his luck and turned every unexpected happening to his favour. When he stumbled on landing and heard his men groan to see him fall, he leapt up with his hands full of earth and cried, 'See, I have England already in my hands!'

Then he chose a strong place to build a fort and sent his cavalry out to terrify the countryside and to bring in food for men and horses. He knew his man and could afford to wait for Harold.

Blazing hill-beacons and hard galloping carried the news to York at the other end of the kingdom. Leaving the wounded behind, Harold broke camp and marched

south at headlong speed. Many of his battered foot-soldiers could not keep up and the northern earls hung back out of disloyalty, but Harold rode on. His army marched at more than thirty miles a day and, as he came, the King gathered soldiers and sent messages for all his troops to join him without delay.

By the evening of October 13th, Harold had reached Sussex. He camped his tired men on a ridge of the Downs, where a single apple-tree, bent by the wind, was a landmark. Less than half the army had arrived. Many were still trudging down from the north, some were coming from the shires and the western fyrd was still a day's march off.

Harold's brothers urged the King to wait. The Normans had had two weeks' rest; his own men had fought a great battle, had twice marched the length of England and were utterly weary. Better to wait; fresh troops would arrive in a day or two and the invaders would be outnumbered by two, three or five to one. Let the Norman Duke cool his heels, they said: burn all the barns and drive off the cattle, so that his men should have to fight on empty bellies.

Harold refused to listen. His people looked to him for protection and he would not burn their farms. Had he not slain the wolf of Norway? Should he not thrash this Norman dog, this son of a tanner's daughter, who had played him false when a guest in his land?

With everything to gain by caution and a kingdom to lose through rashness, Harold's hot temper betrayed him.

At dawn on October 14th, the Normans advanced towards Senlac Hill where Harold offered battle. As usual, the English had dismounted, for they fought on foot, trusting to axe, spear and sword, to a shield-wall, as their fathers had done. They had taken up a strong pos-

ition on the ridge, with the giant housecarls in the
centre, guarding the King and the Royal Standard. On
either side were the thanes and the fighting-men of the
shires, but too many of the troops were ill-armed
peasants hastily drawn into the army while better men
were still marching to serve their King.

The battle began at nine o'clock, when the Norman
archers advanced. The English, who had few bowmen,
bore the hail of arrows and waited stolidly for the real
fighting to begin. Then, when the foreign knights came
up the slope to the shield-wall, they were met by spears,
javelins and showers of stones tied to pieces of wood so
that they were hurled like throwing axes. Those who
reached the shield-wall were assailed by the great English axes that cut through chain-mail as if it were parch-
ment.

A second attack was thrown back. The shield-wall
was unbroken. In front lay piles of Norman dead and
dying, among them Tallifer, the Duke's minstrel, who
had ridden up the slope singing and twirling his sword
like a juggler. By afternoon the Normans were almost
spent.

Suddenly a cry went up that the Duke was slain. His
men wavered and some of the English levies, forgetting
their orders, rushed downhill in joyous pursuit. But William was not dead. Snatching off his helmet to show his
face, he rallied his men, checked their flight and ordered
a ferocious counter-attack. The English who had left
their position were cut down and the Norman cavalry
charged towards the weakened places in the shield-
wall.

Then, as a last throw, the Duke ordered his archers,
who had now replenished their stock of arrows, to fire
high over the heads of his cavalry, so that the arrows fell
like a deadly rain on the English. Harold himself was

struck above the right eye and, from that moment, the spirit of the English army began to falter.

As dusk approached, some of the levies began to steal away and the Norman knights rode through gaps in the wall. Then the English army was broken into knots of valiant warriors who stood their ground and fought back-to-back against a mounted foe who could circle and charge at any point of weakness.

When light faded, the last of the housecarls were still grouped round their slain King and his brothers. Refusing to fly or yield, they swung their axes in stubborn defiance to the end. Even the Normans were awed by such courage.

It was night when the Duke's servants pitched his tent among the slain. In a single day, by luck and daring, he had won a kingdom, for the men who might have led the English to avenge the battle of Senlac Hill lay dead in the darkness with their King.

Index